RHYMES FROM THE HEART

a collection of poems

Tsin Kei

2023

Tsin Kei

Rhymes from the heart : a collection of poems / Tsin Kei. -- Oton, Iloilo :
Faith Claridad, 2023, c2023.

pages ; cm.

ISBN 978-621-06-1054-3 (pb)

978-621-06-1053-6 (pdf)

1. Love poetry, English 2. Philippine poetry (English) --
Collections.

I. Title.

899.210104 PR9550.6 P320230254

Rhymes from the heart

For permissions, email: contact@tsinkei.com
ISBN 978-621-06-1054-3 (Paperback)
ISBN 978-621-06-1053-6 (PDF)

Published by Faith Claridad
Blk. 15, Lot 12, Freesia St., Phase 3, Lumina Homes, Abilay Norte, Oton, Iloilo
(contact@tsinkei.com)

Published in Iloilo, Philippines

TABLE OF CONTENTS

TABLE OF CONTENTS

TABLE OF CONTENTS

Rhymes from the Heart

To all who continue to
live and love

Dear Reader,

Poetry has always been an emotional outlet and an instrument for me to find new meaning in life.

As you flip through the pages, I pray that you'll also realize your worth and love yourself more.

I hope you will keep growing in wisdom and courage.

Regards,

Tsin Kei

A LOVE THAT'S TRUE

When in a dark tunnel you take a walk-through
I'll summon a thousand fireflies for you.

We'll illuminate the world together
With our love so true
                all is brighter.

When tempests come, I'll never worry.
Just hold me in your arms and I'll be okay.

This true love is our shelter
There's nowhere else
                        we could be safer.

A love that's true is what I feel
Even in this deafening muteness, I still hear

My heart screams
            solo tu
Come back now, baby
            te extraño.

TERRIFIED

I'm terrified to believe that you
care.
Of hearing your sweet words,
   I'm scared

I fear of getting used to
        Getting all this affection
      from you

You found me when I was
 broken
 And I can slowly feel the pieces
coming
 together again

But I'm terrified
        to be whole
My heart will die if you left
      after I fell.

A YEAR WITHOUT YOU

A year without
            you feels like
A year of living
            without blood
No matter how much I
      strike
   This heart still won't
pump.

My skin is
            numb
My veins are
         drying up
         Without you in my life
My world is
            paralyzed.

AS LONG AS YOU LOVE ME

As long as you love me
    I'll be your guiding star.
    I will hold you dearly
    No matter where you are.

As long as you love me
    I'll be patient and caring.
    I'll hold on to your hand tightly
    Even when I'm already hurting.

As long as you love me
    Forever is true
    For as long as your heart beats for me
    I shall want nobody but you.

AM I NOT ENOUGH?

Am I not important enough
for you to apologize and stay the
same way?

Am I not loved enough
that you don't want me to be sad
but make me feel that way?

Am I not pretty enough
that you only want to talk with
me
with your fingers?

Am I not delicate enough
that you'll treat me
like cold steel?

LOVE WITHOUT A FACE

Looking up to the twinkling eyes above my head
I see you're not somatic but incorporeal
I've never laid my eyes on you; nothing is to be
depicted
I even know nothing about the bewildering deal

You mean all the world to me but slightly
dubious
I'm clueless if I should remain or depart
My darling, you are capricious
You love me but still tear my heart apart

Ours is a peculiar tale
You are dicey, that's how they understand
It's conspicuous so I never want to tell
I'd never want to be warned

What you are is hours and oceans away
A battle between the present and future for you
and me
Yet, I've been loving you for your grace
Even though you don't have a face.

AT THIS HOUR

At this hour my windows are
                    open
Rested early last night, they're
              broken

Had to get up and take my medicine
      Hard to be sick when all you have is
                    your own
                    skin.

              Wide awake, you join
                    my thoughts
        I ask myself what's the truth

        Should I wake up
              from this dream?
        It's still you I'm thinking.

ATYPICAL

The sun and the earth play hide-and-seek
Plants grow tall or creep
But unlike the mood of an indisputable jerk,
My love for you will never change.

I am a special person
Have Autism for this explanation:
You are my sole fascination;
The absence of yours makes my heart throw tantrums.

I am a poor-sighted creature
I see none of your flaws, just good nature.
I am more than a hearing-impaired girl,
I hear not a censure in the air.

I am handicapped by any means
Yet I still have the best asset.
Gay to manifest this learning disability:
I couldn't learn to "un-love" you no matter what people
say.

CHANGES

When you came into my life I was changed
   I never thought my wings would emerge
Like a caterpillar morphed into a butterfly,
My dreams are great,
        they touch the sky!

You're the only one who could make me
smile at
       silly thoughts,
   I don't mind your awkward jokes when
normally
 they scare me off;
It's strange how those silly things you say
Make it worthwhile
      and make my day.

You took me out of my shell
Every time I open my eyes,
    I am better
Mornings are good with your
   "hello"
Perfect days mean reading your
      "I love you".

Changes are unbearable if for the
      worst
But the transformation caused by you is
   gorgeous
I keep you deeper in my heart with each
passing moment
'coz I was blessed the day we met.

BEING A FRIEND

Being a friend means you listen
when someone needs an ear to confide in

Being a friend means you're feeling
　　　　　someone's grief and pain.

Being a friend means you savor the bliss
　　　for someone's victory and success.

Being a friend means you're ready to embrace
　　　　　and radiate warmth always.

Being a friend means they turn to you
　　　because someone like you is pure and
　　　　　　　true.

COME HERE, HAPPY DREAM!

Come here, happy dream!
Can't you hear me calling your name?

I want to be with you
In my sleep, the only way you will do.

Let me hold your hand
for when I open my eyes,
my own fingers intertwine

Pull me close to you
'coz when I awaken, you're a pillow.

A SMILE

A smile is
what I give
when deep within
is a stuck blade
waiting to cut my being,
my entire soul
into a million pieces
until all that's left of me
are ashes.

DO YOU KNOW WHAT YOU ARE?

My love, do you know that you are
At the bottom
The deepest of
my heart?

No one else could fathom.

I will keep you in the abyss
That no one can
find
There'll be
no egress

You're forever mine.

It mounted my thoughts
You don't know what
you are
You are the one I sought

*But you left me a
scar.*

JUST DON'T

Don't stare at me
Like it's your first time seeing someone
pretty

Don't look at my body
With your malicious eyes piercing
deeply

Don't call out to me
Like we've met each other long before
today

Don't ask me
Where I'm going or what I will do
'Coz it's not for you to know

Don't complain
to me for not responding
Blame yourself for assuming.

EMPTY MORNINGS

I open my eyes and feel a big hole
Something is missing; a part of my soul

I broke into pieces without a fall
I'm clueless about how to complete the
puzzle.

It's hard to get up when you feel like
crying
A sudden tinge of loneliness and longing

I need someone who can understand the
silence
In this life, *I need my own presence.*

ENCHAINED HEART

Moored on this bamboo board masked with sheets
　　This yearning heart of mine fidgets
　　　　'Cause in this warm night of October baker's dozen
　　I've sensed my feelings totally frozen.

What shall I do with this other being?
My mind hovers when it comes to him
For when you join my thoughts, I keep musing
You are the only man my sealed heart would let in.

Why would time swift by when I dream of you?
　　How come when I wake up and wait the motion is slow?
　　　　I wish you know this small fry that is me
　　Will be the apple of your hazel eyes, one day, you'll see.

　　　　I am a hostage drowned in overflowing love,
　　　　　　But I don't want to be ransomed
　　　　For if imprisonment is the mere way to be near you,
　　　　Then I would steal your heart and be enchained too.

FAIRYTALES ARE THE GREATEST SCAMS

I once thought I'd met a man
who would love me like no one else can
I once thought it'll be grand
Just walking together hand in hand.

I once thought the past wounds
would mend
when I met someone
I once thought I'll never cry again
But here's another one.

I once thought happy endings exist
that my happily ever after begins
I once thought I'll be happy in his
kingdom
But I found out fairytales are the
greatest scams.

FANTASY

This heart
desires to be with you,
My breath, my beat, my love in toto

Heisting a heart that's mine,
Could you jump off my mind?

In the nocturnal solitude
thoughts must be still too

Yet, princely images of you my mind
projects
I am struck by a love hex;
it couldn't be just a jest

Reaching out for the premium
For your love, special attention

Though, I know I belong to the
rabble,
Winning your heart is possible.

FISH

After the heaven's curtains
                eclipsed the daylight
The bed carries my weight
                Indian sit
With both hands folded upright
                I envisage
a mortal's silhouette

The two unsealed windows on his face
                flicker
Like stars shining some light
        on life below
And his smile
        is the sun engulfing the shiver
Consoling any chilled fellow

My eyes caught his beatific trait
                And I ascertain
        Submerged in this sea so quiescent
    He resembles my greatest dream

    Before I rest my head on
                mellow cotton
        I'll grip his fin and hold it tight
I'll blow wishing candles in
        orison,
May this vertebrate swim his way
                into my life.

FEARS

I am not sure if you still remember
When I told you about my fear
Told you I was scared of falling
Because ***falling in love can be
heartbreaking***.

I was frightened when I realized
That I wanted you despite the distance
For months I had my doubts
I wanted to clear your memories but they're
out and about.

Your love makes me happier
But no matter how I think about being
bolder,
My fear creeps in out of the blue
Now, ***I fear losing you***.

GHOST

I have once loved a man—
   Who loved me more;
I talked to him with my
hands
  Just right inside my wall.

I thought that quarrels were a
normal twist,
    When a fairytale arose;
Until he cut his wrist,
  Now I'm in love with a ghost.

HOLD ON

Take courage my darling, amidst the chaos
For today, we must stand against the storm
One day, our paths shall cross
If we vow to hold on

We may be seas and oceans apart
But I hold thy love in my heart
When thou art down please think of me
Thy life is never empty

My heart yearns for the day
I will be gazing into thine eyes directly
This longing shall live in me
Till the moment when I'm with thee.

HOPE YOU COULD SEE

Incipient now are my feelings for thee
Love—I could not bestow on other guys
unreservedly,
Only with thee, I long to experience pure
camaraderie,
Versifying what this heart yearns to vent yet is
laborious for me.

Euphonious is thy voice to my hearing sense;
Yes—though aloft, I reach in this cadence
Owning thine heart is my utmost wish
"Untouchable you" is a phrase I truly detest.

Defiance is everything that keeps me strong
An anadem I put my head on
Vividly, the future tells per se;
I am your virtuous destiny,
Dear, I hope you could see.

Jerk I'd be in their eyes
Absurd are for them, my desires
Meshing with thee may seem like a hopeless dream
Eccentrically loving thee might be a hushed scream;
Soundless as it is though, I faithfully care deep
within.

HOURS APART

Your goodnights
My good mornings,
You sup in my dreams
Lock your windows in my
daylight.

Your endings
My beginnings
Hours away
Will we meet one day?

I MISS YOUR PRESENCE

When I'm surrounded by
many,
It's you I wish to see.
Each day is empty,
If you're not here with
me.

I don't feel like playing a
song,
And my guitar is out of
tune
I'm out of words to write,
'cause it doesn't seem right.

You took away my inspiration;
Your silence removed my
motivation,
Now I feel black and blue,
Breathing is never the same
without you.

I WISH YOU COULD SEE

You might not be able to
comprehend,
How I keep holding on to us;
But each time the wound mends
I ponder that *all we need is trust*

I can't fathom how you feel
Why you do the things you do
      But with this love so real
I know we can get it through

I wish you could see
That even if the whole world lets you
down
      I will be here to stay
I'll always be around

I hope soon enough you will realize
You are the apple of my eye
      I wish you could see
You'll always be the best for me.

7,650 MILES

I feel your
            presence
under the twinkling dots

They
    are your sparkling eyes
from a distance

You
      may be miles away
Still, I breathe in
          your breath
every day.

I WANT TO KNOW

I want to know how it
feels
  To be sitting alongside
you
With our intertwined
fingers
    Like it's always new

I want to sense your
warmth
  As the gentle breeze
kisses me
To stay safe in your arm
    Holding me tightly

Want to hear my heart
beating loudly
  Staring into the windows
of your soul
To read your lips saying
softly
  I am the one you'll always
fall for.

IF OUR WORLDS COLLIDE

Being with you will never be faux
Joining hands with you will be a go
Just like the sough by my side
I could hear you whisper gently if our worlds
collide

I would never lose heart again
Even if I keep harping on the same string
Presage could no longer have its turn
If in my present world, you are around

I would no longer have a face as long as a fiddle
For a sole smile from you gives my heart a tickle
Every moment with you would be a roller coaster
ride
Love would spin me around if our worlds collide

A knock-out man like you is few-and-far-between
In you, I found a better paradise under heaven
Your absence makes my heart grow fonder
If our worlds collide, I dare say I would be crazier.

INVISIBLE

You said you felt lonely,
        Kept saying you were tired
while I waited patiently.
  My heart rips open
Blood gushes out, *I'm broken.*

  Am I an invisible wind?
   Or a drip that washes away in the
rain?
 I just want you to see me again
    I miss the old times we've
       been in.

I'VE FALLEN FOR A HIGH STAR

Last night,
I went out to meet the asteroids,
   Telling them my hush-hush,
 I could not avoid.
I would never want my petition become
     null and void.
Then as I talked to my Father
     Right under
a light-speckled crater,
The pure air blew a fresh shiver.

I could always tell Him
 that I always want to look up to heaven
And reach a glimpse of
 what I dream
But before I'm done, it fired
     right above my head;
Starstruck
as it went on,
     my wish was late.
I've fallen for a high star and was
desperate.

JOURNAL

In happiness we're hand in hand
Soothe me, bitterness is fat;
Thank you, my associate in grief
and song,
To me alone, you belong.

Daylight for me isn't perfect;
It refused to be terrific
Yet, I'm blessed by an
imperfection like you
For you are faithful and true.

I'm glad you're my friend
Both in loss and gain,
You help me unclench,
You lift my mood when I need it.

JUST LOOK BACK

Take a step back and turn around
    Look into my eyes
No one else, but you
    have found
Where the brightest star lies

Others were searching for so long
But for you, the light years were
 abridged
You've captured your star
    with just a song
You gave me light
  that couldn't be effaced

Look at what you've done!
  You made my
  prosaic day a sophisticated one
I'm getting used to the fervid
fun you have at hand,
When you're gone
  I'll be standing
    frozen on an arid land

Can I ask you to stay?
I vow to behave in a proton way
I'll be your guide beginning today
If only, you knew
I've been here with you
from a thousand miles away.

LIKE STREAMS

Tumults saunter to the north;
Bewilderment strolls to the south,
Far-and-wide encumbrances gush
Goaded by increasing rush.

But let them not
Flood through the threshold of your heart
Trap them in the abysmal roots instead
Of great courage you had planted.

Great mistakes emerge out of the blue
Prying the darkness on you
And you find it hard to wend,
For your aching feet won't mend.

Problems flow like streams;
Once you've carried away, you'll lose your dreams.
But embrace your faith tight
The time has not yet come to lose a fight.

Set your view aloft
With recalcitrance, move forth
Turn the faucet off.
Each eye drop counts.

LOST

You might not feel
the numbing pain
but *I can*
each time my eyes
are open.
You might not see
but *I am*
running in circles;
lost my way,
my life.

LOVE IS

Love is pure and it is
   blind,
Of imperfections, it'll
   never mind.

Love is the cure for any
     pain,
You shouldn't lose,
   only gain.

Love is selfless and full of
     grace,
It illuminates the
   darkest days.

Love is accepting someone's
   weaknesses,
Helping them unleash their
   greatest *strengths*.

Love is forgiving
   after a fight,
Not staying mad when you
sleep
     at night.

Love is stronger than
    physical desires,
It lives on even after one
    dies.

LOVESICK RHYMES

I gawk at his countenance,
By his beam, my heart
is replete with recalcitrance,
Chiding myself for being goosy
My head rebels but I'm giddy.

Lost in a labyrinth of "what ifs"
I embrace mirth but not sensing
complacent;
My bohemian soul is not
Incessantly vivacious;
She's baffled by the world
So humongous.

I'm in the dreg of my day;
My grotesque self is grappling with
anxiety,
I need no snide physiognomy,
But desire pure equanimity.

He's my dream that's not yet true;
My gregarious ramification
But he offers blurring innuendo,
If I'm his heart's gratification.

LOVING YOU

When I met you,
I was *smitten*
You made my list of standards
totally *forgotten,*
Even though I sometimes feel
broken
Loving you
is still the best thing I've ever
chosen

I never thought
I'd ever *try*
To do things that make me
shy
But loving you means
silly words don't
matter
You always make my heart
flutter

You make me alive and
merry
With every little sweet thing
you say
Loving you made me forget my
ideal man
'coz babe, you're *the best* in the
land.

MAGNETS

A pair of magnets
is what we are
two different worlds
colliding
but
not collapsing
opposite sides
attracting each other
miles apart
but drawn together.

MIRRORS

My breath of life escapes
        To join the smoke coverings
That jailed the smile of Sol
            Over my freezing soul

    Reflections that hit
This floor don't leave a hint
        Of what will be mine
        If tomorrow shall ever shine

    What's the use of these mirrors
      If you can't see what's yours?
By looking at it, I can only see
shadows
        A glimpse of the clouds'
unshed sorrows

        Mirror, mirror on the floor
        Can I ask you a favor?
        Please stop flowing away
        I want to see if I'm pretty.

MOMENTS

The moment I open my eyes,
there you go
Thoughts of you emerge like some
bubbling shampoo
You're the early light from my
window
You stir me up in a
new glow

The moment I touch the floor,
there you go
Images of you spring
like bamboo
You're the weight I tip from
toe to toe
You carry my love
each day anew

The moment I sip from my cup
there you are
Your words remind me like
an alarm
I taste the bitter sap
sensing you from afar
I don't have my heart in my hand
without your warmth.

MY BEE

My bee
where hast thou flown?
I sought for thee
from night till dawn
Thou hast
left me
alone
I know not where to go
for thou art
my home.

Why doth thou
not hearest?
What I wanted since
December
To me thy honey
thoughts
thou sharest
I beseech thee
pardon me
from this fear.

NUMB

There you go again,
sending messages of affection
Letting me know how special I am
There you go again,
seeking my attention
Making me feel
how numb I am

You're a bee trying to woo a rose
But I don't know how to respond
to it.
My prickling thorns could
leave your heart with wounds;
I fear you can't escape

It's not that I'm too choosy
I'm just looking for
something I don't even know
And telling you is not easy
That this thing I look for
is not in you

How could I get rid of
my thorny heart's sting?
I don't want to hurt you
How could I say I love you
without pretending?
I'm not hit by Cupid's arrow.

NONEXISTENCE

I wish to
disappear immediately
Like a
bubble that pops
and forgotten
easily
If nobody knows
I existed before
No one
will be bothered
by my fall.

It'll be better if I
evaporate
into thin air
That's more
preferable than living
in hell
I wish I could
turn into gas
It's much better
if I forget
who I was.

OBLIVION

Four months without a word
   Can't tell if I'm
      lonely or bored
Should I bury you in oblivion?
   I'm scared of moving on.

      I know I told you to take
       your time
      To mend yourself
       be fine
      But is it worth the wait?
      Of coming back,
   do you even think?

  My heart chooses to believe
You will look for me in
   the end
Yet I fear I'll get used to your
     absence
And will no longer want your
   presence.

ON THE FENCE

I was looking
for the purpose
of my breath

A lot of
queries
waiting
for the truth

Grilling my brain
about
how long
I should wait
For an answer
to come forth

I saw
 people
living well
And I came
to. recall
How I
used to be
 better

Now
I just
tumble.

Tsin Kei

ONE DAY, YOU'LL SEE

I don't need
another show
Why worry
about me?
Don't you have
enough
of your own?

Learn
to wait, my friend
One day you'll see
me standing
at the top
While you
tumble in a snap

Be careful
what you do
life is an echo
One day,
you will reap
 what you sow.

ONLY YOU

The first time we said "Hi,"
 I thought you're only
passing by
        I didn't anticipate
My once guarded heart
        would open the gate
Only you could break my
walls
 easily
Now, I want you every day

        I guess I
haven't told you enough
How I see no one else
 but you
        You are
a diamond in the rough
That makes my heart glow

If this is my
        last chance
I think you should know
I'll stay with you
 till the end of the dance
        'coz in my heart
there's only you.

OUR VIRTUAL LOVE STORY

I'm thinking about
nuestra historia
Would like to
open my eyes from
la fantasía

For when they're shut
completely
You are
my reality.

Why can't this be easy?
Left me hanging,
por qué?
Where are you?
Can't you hear my heart
saying
te amo?

PERFECT PAIR

When love
is sailing
I'll be the quay for thy ship

When love
is singing
I'll be the highest note of thy music

Thou art the key for my
door's lock
Inaccessible is my heart
with thine absence

Thou art the most comfortable
footwear
in the rack
Without thee
I couldn't go to any place

If love
is about writing
Thou art every word in my
write-up

If love
is about dancing
Thou art every move in the
step-up

Thou art the ink of
my marker
The pencil for my sharpener
We are meant to
be together
One won't work without the
other.

POEM FOR YOU

I want to write a poem
To let you know how I really
feel
Yet here I am trying hard to
catch on
Why is it so challenging to tell?

This thing that we have is
peculiar
Who knows it is possible to love
from afar?
Now I know, love moves in
mysterious ways
You came to my life at a time I
expected it the least

We are two different worlds
crashing with mistrust
But we found love instead of
falling apart
This time, I am giving you my
heart
And I am not taking it back.

PROMISES

I promise to
 always talk
To God
about you

I will
slowly
walk
So anytime
you may follow

But please
 promise me
You will combat
 the solitariness
Stay
firm and rosy
Because
you're
 my cheerfulness.

PUZZLED

Wedged on this seat for quite some time,
Got a lot of things in my head yet have
nothing to write;
It's like having the drive but uninspired
Or maybe it's the other way; puzzled is my
mind.

Mixed-up are the thoughts in my brain
I just wanted to tell you something
But I could not spot the words,
My mind has gone astray in another
world.

I wonder if you think of me;
Do you comprise me when you pray?
I marvel what my life would seem to be
When you've crossed my way.

Whether or not in your dreams you have
seen
That I am the one you've been waiting,
I discern I have found the precise omen;
Years from now, I foresee
You'll share with me your family name.

QUANDARY

Laid my head down with
some ire as my pillow
Brain is enigmatized;
Saw quagmire peeking out
my shut window
Heart is traumatized.

Bliss-filled darkness,
Tragic brightness;
Should I let go or stay?
Every trice is a quandary.

The harder I reckon
Of this as a fantasy
The more the senses beckon
This could be the reality.

NIGHT MUSING

Here I am trying to
decipher,
Does your dwelling in my
head turns me into a
dawdler?
For this nocturnal glee the
stars dazzle over me;
When daybreak steps in,
becomes foggy.

Can't dragoon my cardiac
instinct to my neural truth,
An infinite battle between
maturity and youth;
A tireless shift of scenes
from the fantasy I mold
To the prickling reality I try
to shove.

SKY OF LOVE

Took steps with your tunes in my ears
Going to and fro with a taciturn pace
Green, gold, pale red and beige
Till I've memorized all shades of the
garden leaves.

When you went away
Your luggage tugged off a part of me
Now, I could never give luck to any of
them
You've packed the sole heart of my
system.

Dusk isn't a thing of beauty
Not when no constellations are blinking
brilliantly
To remind me we are under the same sky
Perfectly together—
 You and I.

SOMEDAY, SOMEHOW

Lying wide awake
Thoughts of you are hard to break
My skin's hoping to feel your breath
Beneath these dancing curtains.

The moonlight resting next to me
Makes me lonely;
I gaze at the round eye above
Wishing it's your smile I see, my love.

Tonight, the moon stretches out its
arms
But I long to only feel your warmth;
If you're not just passing by,
Someday, somehow, you'll be by my
side.

SONNET

Could I ever find an egress
From this unlovely town?
I am so sick of this unfriendly place;
It does not feel like home.
I ran down towards the pond;
Nothing—the fishes were long dead,
So I climbed my way up to the highland
But lo! The plants have withered.
I sat on a cliff bearing hue and cry,
The snakes gibed at me with hissing sound;
But if I feasted on them, I'd die
I stood up instead, stomping them to homeward
bound
Packing my clothes, I'm ready to leave,
Time to move out from this dark cave.

Sparks of Hope

Worry not, my distant star
I view your dim sparkles from afar
Cold, they may seem
But I ideate, someday they'll gleam.

Patience isn't my truth
And my gaiety is out of youth
Yet I'll glue my heart to a corner
To keep it yours forever.

Breathe all you wish
Shut the doors till you replenish,
I know when the hour is right
The shadows would fade as fireflies ignite.

A ray of hope is all we quest
Each day a kiss of prayer sent
I'll watch you be freed from the sky
And catch you with a loving smile.

STAYING WITH YOU

Is it too much to ask
If I want to hold you in the dark?
For I am very scared of the breeze
That blows away your gaze.

I don't want to halt
The thought of always holding your
hand
Every day with you is paradise
So let's freeze here from sundown till
sunrise.

STILL YOU

How can I
Advance
When my heart
Still beats for the past?

I laugh with him
but my feelings are wailing,
I spend time with him
but my thoughts are flying
Far away
To find you
In a place I've never been.

SUPERSTAR

Glaring at heaven above
Constantly longing for my far-
off love
I was searching for a star with
peculiar spark;
To the rhythm of its light I
desire to hark.

Sat I in a garden of green mists
Embraced by the yellow-
blooming sugary scents
At 7:11 as the golden ball shone
up so high
Behind the thin smoke a tail of
brightness flew by.

A shooting star it was!
Such sight charged my chest to
pound fast;
Before it could fade to where
ashes are
I whispered to be thy girl, my
superstar!

THE BEST LOVE

The best love doesn't come and go.
It stays and grows with you.
The best love isn't insensitive to how you feel.
It cares and always shares.
The best love isn't about insisting on one's beliefs.
It respects differences.
The best love isn't rude.
It has an understanding that's broad.
The best love isn't suffocating.
It encourages a free human being.
The best love doesn't leave someone feeling blue.
It fills one's world with a rainbow.
The best love I thought I'd never know,
Is the one I found in you.

THE CAGE

This is my world
With six corners around
Where the sun and the stars stand beside
each other,
For life and death are bestfriends forever.

I am sleeping with clouds over my bed,
And sea creatures glowing up the pool above
my head.
But the soft fur could devour only the
tranquility of their light,
While she purrs my lullaby through the night.

In this cage, I am a bird of changing hues;
With feathers soaked in black ink for
rhyming words,
A beak washed in pure white for humming
melodies;
And claws dyed in a rainbow for painting
images.

In my world, there's no horizon;
Furniture keep strolling in every direction
When a broom
Gives me a renovated home.

THE CHAMELEON

Here I am, keeping myself
unseen
Under a rock I call my home.
I am not someone forsaken,
Just someone wanting to be
alone.

I try to change my color
Wherever the current flows
Yet, I discreetly ask for a favor
That the sun won't reveal my
skin when it glows.

I saw a hawk flew by
And hid myself in fear again;
I wish I could also soar high
Be myself without blending in.

May this dilemma end as the
sun goes down,
That I may stand on my own
Because I'm sick of being a
reptile;
I'm so done trying to please
everyone on this isle.

Tsin Kei

THE SPECKLED BUTTERFLY

Mourn with the speckled
butterfly
Who was once a flawless
caterpillar,
Now drinking on flower-cups as
the sun is high;
She was once nibbling her own
roof during a storm signal.

While the other insects adored
her beauty,
They know not of her
imperfection.
They sang her praises gently;
But her bee-dad buzzed about
her spots all afternoon.

The bee who was her adoptive
father,
Kept nagging at her scornfully,
Anything she did wouldn't
matter;
Not until she could produce
honey.

THERE'S NOTHING I CAN DO

You say you love me so much
When it can't be seen in the actions you show
I keep believing it though you're out of touch
I care for you and *there's nothing I can do.*

Each time you tell me you are ill
I want to dash across the globe to see you
But it's not easy, I would marvel
So, I just pray for you coz *there's nothing else I can do.*

Even if you make me feel unappreciated, I'll try to
understand
I would tell myself I am talking to depression
and not with you
My heart is bleeding but my love for you is grand
So, I will cry silently coz *there's nothing I can do.*

THINGS I LOVE ABOUT YOU

I love the way you look at me
Making me feel like I'm
The only maiden you see

I love how you laugh at my jokes
'coz even if they're silly
You appreciate my efforts

I love it when you say
You love me more
For it completes my day.

THINKING OF YOU

I just woke up from my reverie
Discovering this diaphaneity:
You've made me truly smitten;
And the proof is every poem for you I have
written
Each time my mind becomes your den

I am a renegade
My priorities are getting lopsided
I am an angel with a rakish halo;
My thoughts now becoming askew,
They always point at you

By looking at you, I got aghast
Now this feeling had left me in a serious
nonplus;
However, I am ironclad,
By dwelling in my mind, you made me glad
And it's out of my hand

Even if I'll see the dreg of your character one
day,
The love I have for you won't meander away.
If you ever become rowdy, I promise not to be
crabby.
It will forever be a feather in my cap to be your
one and only.

TORN

I'm torn between 'yes' and 'no'
'stay' or 'go'
For I'm satiated by sorrow
But when I see the sadness in
your eyes,
I couldn't stay as cold as ice.

My feelings are shattered
In more than two,
I'm broken but my heart
goes out to you
I'm unsure whom I feel this
pain for
Is it for me or for you more?

TWO YEARS AND FOREVER

I looked up to the half-full bulb above
Under this roof, I hope that you see
The moon-made halo which
mesmerized me.

I'm trying to breathe your warmth in
the cold air;
Imagining you are right here,
Because each time I look up, I could
feel you're near,
I've been loving you for two years and
forever.

I smiled as I prophesied all of our
tomorrows
It's the mere way to conceal the
sorrows
How I wish I could just hit the
forward button
So in a blink, I could have your hand
to hold on.

I've been doing this for quite a long
time,
And it's a tragic addiction of mine;
Yet, even if I had known that waiting
could bring pain,
I would still choose to love you for
two years and forever again.

UNEXPECTED LOVE

I never thought
I would meet someone who
Is more than what I needed

I never expected
To fall in love with someone who
Loves me more than I wanted

I never knew
I would find someone who
Truly cares

But now I'm sure
You're the answer
To my prayers.

UPSET

It's 12:30 AM and I can't sleep
I opened a bottle of soju and
gulped it
I wish to be drunk
to fall asleep and forget this
mess
And if I throw up, I hope my
sorrow goes down the drain
with it

I don't know what to do
If I go to bed, I'll cry thinking
about you
About how I don't feel loved
these days
Because I'm upset and you
don't seem to notice

I sulk and hope you'll coax me
But you avoid me instead so I
feel terribly lonely
You say sorry but it's an empty
word
Coz when I forgive you
everything is the same
I'll be okay for a moment and
get upset again.

WHERE I BELONG

Missing you so badly, I can't catch on
When it comes to you I don't want to back
down;
Obsessed of thinking that I'm the one you want
to be with,
That everything I dream of is in the wind;
Can't keep down of minding of you all along,
To you, my thoughts belong.

I'm afraid to open my mouth and be loquacious;
Fear to slip my tongue and dig you out of my
subconscious,
Because what I feel for you is atypical;
You have infected me with a love so hysterical,
And it's amazing how you tuned my guitar on.
It's for you, I sing my love song.

Reaching out to you is not against the clock,
And I'll keep it on, hook it on a rock;
If God would one day redden the street lamp,
I swear, I could not just jump at;
The piece will be half-baked if my affection is
wrong,
It's for you alone that I'm writing this poem.

WITHOUT YOU

The world's dark on a sunny day,
It's sweltering when it's rainy;
The weather turns silly
When there's no 'you and me'

It's hard to fall asleep without your
goodnights
Mornings are awful without your light
Things just don't seem right
Without you in my sight

Poems aren't interesting,
Comedies turn boring;
Love songs suddenly sound dull
'coz without you here, my life is null.

WORLDS APART

I could not bring to mind the exact
jiffy
When my heart fell and broke in
moiety;
Though between us there is a mighty
wall,
The air still blows love through a wee
hole
And with the night sky as our
intercom,
I'd leave messages in modicum;
You may not hear the words precisely
But I pray that the warmth is
transmitted to you instantly

We are antonyms in a lot of ways
And it is hard to sing along
But I'm going to use my head tone to
reach your keys
So we could let the music play on;
'Cause heaven knows how much I
care,
To tear the partition down, I would
dare
I'd kick this wall till I'm lame
If that's what it takes to reach my
dream.

You're the Reason

I'm crackling my head only to scribble a few rhymes
I'm staying wide awake just to mind a few lines
Everything this poetaster is doing,
You're the reason why I keep going.

I'm struggling to stretch a muscle,
Never minding if I broke an ankle
The reason why I want to be an epitome of beauty
Is for you to remember the day you'd meet me.

I'll be fibbing
If I'd say that I'm far from being apprehensive
But you're the reason why I keep on believing
Even if the future is not pellucid.

My feelings for you is in any length but ephemeral;
You're the reason I hanker to welcome each day
My faith in you is in any size but infinitesimal;
Because you bring out the best in me.

SEPARATION

The absence of words,
Needs more than just familiarity
The silence of sounds,
Gives more than just tranquility

Separation caused us to
Gain placidity
No arguments between us two,
Just deficiency

I desire a disarray of thoughts
Guess that's better
I'd rather entertain doubts
Just to have you here.

GIVE ME SOME TIME

I didn't want to show
How I liked the way you held my hand
But if you only knew
Maybe you would understand
I'm just asking you to *give me some time.*

I might've tried to hide
That I liked how you brushed my hair with
your fingers
But I felt the chills deep inside
When you said how soft my face is
But still, I ask you to *give me some time.*

I know I'm sometimes rude to you
'Cause I am conscious with the people
around;
I'm not used to this kind of scenario
When someone makes me feel safe and
sound
So please *give me some time.*

If you only know, I'm just afraid
Afraid to fall in love and make a mistake
I would want to see some signs if it's really
you
Before I declare we are the reversed of NO
So *give me some more time.*

FORWARD

It's a slippery slope
At dawn lost, every rope
But this time with a ladder
Stepping on, would I utter:
History may print dark trails
Still, I would never look back with wails
Even if everything is stripped away
God remains in me

People may gossip whatever they think
of me
Outer person, anyway, is all they see
Can't cause me to ululate
I got inner peace,
Their umbrages, I'll forgive instead.

I DON'T WANT YOU

I don't want your love to be like the
wind
Sometimes strong, sometimes weak
I don't want your affection to be like
beverage
That might be sweet or acrid.

I don't want your attention to be like a
sail
That changes course depending on the
weather
I don't want you as a lesson to learn
But a treasure I could keep forever.

MY DARLING

Darling, tell me if you truly care
Are you imagining me
leaning on your shoulder?
No one else joins my mind
It is you my heart desires.

Every time you are far
Lovesickness wants war
Would you mind staying for a while?

All I long for is your sugar smile
Nothing is more charming than your
face
Gaily, I'd get stuck in your embrace.

AFTER YOU GO

So it's true
How people remember
Your value
When you aren't together.

You get appreciation
You cannot feel
You get a declaration
You cannot hear.

The world will know you
Only after you go
But when you are breathing
They don't see anything.

MR. SINGER

He is a prince for every young lady;
Flowing with charm and beauty.
I fell for every rhythm he would play.
Now, that is the voice of an angel;
So, what more can I tell?

He is as bright as the sun
With a ray reaching this Earth
To melt my frail heart from a distance.
Through music, he shines just like a superstar;
His melodies warm my heart from afar.

I WISH YOU KNEW

I wish you knew something
Something akin to my occult feeling
A mystery words couldn't exactly express
An emotional splendor without an escape.

I'm mind-traveling as I ramble
Now enthralled by your effulgence
But a glimpse of your prestigious world
 makes me feel so small;
In a vast ocean, I couldn't see my
existence.

This pounding in my chest is an enigmatic
sense;
I'm falling for a man from a remote place.
It's like dreaming of a star from outer space
You're typically out of my reach.

I wish I could let you know how I feel
I wish you knew I want this for real;
I wish I could let you lucidly see
You'll share a brilliant future with me.

ON MY OWN

All alone, thinking
Of the bygone with your presence
I can't halt my eyes leaking waters
Revoking the memories

I wavered to show
Now, I want to make it known to
you
Those three last words I told you
I meant them—it's true!

Only at first I minded
Should I, could I, would I mourn
For insoluble was I enough to carry
on
Misty eyes—but why now?
Had I not proclaimed I've moved
on?

PARTS OF THE PAST

Declared you fell for me
I signed in it with no vacillation
Hilarity almost drowned me
As I dived in your enthusiasm.

But as the arrow ticked at a rapid pace,
Warmth departed from your face.
Amid the blooming faithfulness in my
part;
You burned the mud, cracked my heart.

Oh, how I miss the way we were
In your wrist you wore my silver name so
dear
But the merriments I once fought to last
They are all now in the past.

THE FEELING I HATE

Oh this feeling that I
feel!
This is so unexpectedly
real,
Don't know how we got
here,
'cause now, I think I am
beginning to care.

Why do I feel conscious
when thou art near me?
But I feel cozy sitting
beside thee;
Why am I restless of thy
presence?
But it feels half-baked if
I don't see thy face.

THE LAST THING I'D EVER WANT TO BE

You kept on saying
You can't take me off your mind
And that you can't help staring
No matter how hard you tried.

I don't even know what you are to me anymore
Am not certain whether you're just a friend or
more
For all the kindness I have left within me
Being an antagonist is the last thing I'd ever want
to be.

I'm sorry if I made you baffled
I never meant to do that
I hope you could end the battle
Between your head and heart.

I despise being in this situation again
I don't want to color outside the margin
Days like these make me feel uneasy
Being a relationship-wrecker is
the last thing I'd ever want to be.

THY CHOICE

Ask me not if thou shall woo
For I never say 'yes' or 'no'
Come hither if thou art
fascinated
Come with thy courage all
gathered

Coyly, thou say "hi,"
But here I sit, letting go a sigh
Till I wonder over again
What must've kept thee from
talking

I tried to explain what I
meant
But thou never caught on
I wanted to say it wouldn't
hurt to wait
But thou hast claimed thy
doom

Do not wait for my signal
I'm not closing the portal
Never wait to hear my voice
Because walking in is all thy
choice.

THE LAST LETTER

Dear Pretty,

You were a good person
Pure of heart, not asking for a reason
Whenever of what you want you were deprived;
Calling it a day hadn't lured your mind.
It's esoteric why I'm scribbling this
Can't find the right words, my thoughts is in the
abyss;
Why does life bring so much mess?
It simply fades away the people it must cherish.
So much is to be remembered from you
History that'll be left as you go;
Your presence is gone
But we'll treasure the beauty of what you have
done.
In every thing, there's a season
Agent M., you've done your mission;
Now, you'll vanish from our view
But there's no oblivion of you.
To you, we say farewell
And there's much to dry up—the tears
But this wouldn't last forever
So rise up to heaven, be our angel
Seek for your soul's peace,
We'll see you there someday.

Cherishing the memories,

Your first love

PERFECT FOR YOU

Of her, you are thinking,
About her, you've been
searching.
Wanted to meet your girl
But you know right
She's just out there
out here
somewhere

Let those damsels go.
None of them, is the kind of
perfect for you
She is far
in a long-distance
relationship
In the future
with you.

With you as the prince
I want a fairytale
for me in the end,
Just keep holding on,
I'll be there with you
soon.

OH, WHY WON'T YOU

Oh, why won't you take a
glance?
    So you will have a chance
To see at least
     What might be the best

Oh, why won't you head turn
back?
   To find what you've sought,
'Cause I should be the one you
look at
  To love you without a second
        thought

Oh, why won't you come
closer?
    So that you could hear
Your heartbeat racing more
  Like you've never felt before

Oh, why won't you try to get
 To know me better, a little bit
 The one you're searching for,
    you'll soon realize
Is already standing right before
      your
     very eyes.

IRREGULAR BEAT

Filling my ears with rhythmic noise
Trying to be free from my brain's voice;
For if my mind revolves in a world so
solemn,
I can't help but remember your cognomen.

I beg you to leave my thoughts alone,
Take them not as you head home.
I am not comfortable of having this beat
aloud;
Though I would have wanted you to be
around.

This is just too much;
Do not make me transgress my own
standards,
I want to be the one who's behind in years;
Not just someone younger as it seems.

Of feeling guilty, I don't want to;
I am against this irregular beat I feel for
you,
So walk away without looking back at me;
I'd get confused if those eyes, I would see.

IF YOU WOULD ONLY LET ME BE

If I were a clown
I'll make you smile when you're down.
I'll turn into mornings, all your dark nights
If you would only let me be your light.

If I were the wind
I'd blow away your sorrows, send their end
I won't let your feet hit the ground;
If you would only let me be the wings to fly you
around.

If I were Cupid's bow and arrow
I'll strike a pure heart, make it fall for you
I'll put "U" and "I" together
If you would only let me rearrange the letters.

If I were a song,
I'll play melodies of affection to you all along.
I'll twist your every frown into an exquisite smile;
If you would only let me walk down the aisle.

DAYS AFTER WE SAY "HI"

It's only been days since we
said hello
I started to open up
and felt comfortable with you
But when I asked if we could
talk on video
You said your phone was bad,
though you'd love to
I believe you don't want me to
see you
and I'm not buying your alibi
I wonder if you will still reply,
Things are now messy
just days after we said "hi."

DILEMMA

What did you do to me?
How did you make me feel this way?
I don't want to fall for you;
That is the last thing I ever want to do.

You are not the kind of person
To whom I want to entrust my heart
with
But should I still go on with my
reasons
When the feelings have been
reciprocated?

Oh no! This can't be!
I can't believe that I fall in love easily.
I know this is not something new,
But I'm really afraid to commit to you.

Maybe, I should put the blame on
gravity
Which makes me float when you are
near
Or should it be on me
for thinking so much if you're not
here?

My brain says no
But my heart beats I like you too
Now, I don't really know what to do,
It's hard to choose between the two.

To all the boys I used to love

To all the boys
I used to love
don't worry, I'm not
 mad.
I was hurt but you
just
played your part
to teach me
that
I deserve better
than what we had.